Speak German Today!

A conversation course on cassette for visitors to Germany

Hugo's Language Books Ltd, London

This edition
© 1987 Hugo's Language Books Ltd
All rights reserved
ISBN 0 85285 116 2

Written by

Winfried Peter Reichwald

*Facts and figures given in this book were
correct when printed. If you discover any
changes, please write to us.*

Printed in Great Britain by
Buckland Press Ltd, Barwick Road,
Dover, Kent

Preface

How many people have gained a background knowledge of German yet still find themselves floundering in a German shop or any other situation where they have to say a little more than 'How much is it?' and 'Thank you'? Are you one of those who has been through a home study or classroom course in the language but still cannot master the conversational element as easily as you had hoped?

The thirteen conversations on this cassette recording are designed to bridge that gap. They assume a fair knowledge of German grammar, but all are applicable to the everyday situations in which the visitor to Germany is most likely to find him- or herself . . . buying food or clothes, ordering meals, asking for directions and so on.

An effort has been made to keep the language colloquial, corresponding to what one actually hears in Germany, and so contracted forms and conversational turns of phrase have been used by the native German speakers on this recording. The content of each dialogue, while remaining realistic, has been carefully devised to provide the learner with plenty of practical information about the German way of life, especially in cases where it differs from our own.

Contents

Introduction

How to use the course

Each conversation has been recorded twice. First, you will hear the speakers talking at a normal rate; listen to one of these complete conversations several times before progressing to the second rendering. In this, there is a pause before the visitor's part in the dialogue — giving you time to say the words yourself before hearing them on the tape. You can do this either by working from memory or by reading the part from the text. To make it clear which part is yours, we have indicated this in the text by the symbol • against each appropriate entry.

You may wish to record yourself on another tape and then compare your pronunciation with that of the original speaker; this will give you practice in both formulating what you want to say and understanding what is said to you in reply.

The notes and English translation

The notes are intended to make your stay in Germany easier and more enjoyable by drawing your attention to certain German customs, as well as to linguistic features. Each marginal number in the German conversation refers to italicised words in the following sentence; these are explained at the end of the piece, under *Fußnote*. Try to understand these German notes first, before referring to the English version under the heading *Notes*. You will see that these follow directly, instead of coming after the English translation of the conversations. The reference numbers are shown only in the German dialogues because the notes often refer to a feature which has no equivalent in English.

The English translations of the conversations appear at the end of the book; these are as literal as possible, but we have given a free translation where a literal one would sound strange to the English ear.

Care of your cassette

Just in case you've forgotten how carefully a tape needs to be handled, here are some gentle words of warning! Do not switch your player from "play" to "rewind" or "fast forward" without stopping the tape first of all, and ensure that there is no slack tape between the two holes of the cassette before you insert it into your player. If there is, the tape may double back and become stretched, crumpled or broken by getting wound round the machine's capstan. To avoid this, simply insert a pencil (preferably one with flat sides) or your finger into one or other of the holes and turn the sprocket in the appropriate direction to take up the slack between the two hubs. Do not over-tighten the tape, for obvious reasons!

An der Hotelrezeption

EMPFANGSDAME		Guten Morgen, mein Herr. Sie wünschen bitte?
• GAST	1	Guten Morgen. Ich hätte gern ein *Doppelzimmer*.
EMPFANGSDAME		Wie lange wollen Sie bleiben?
• GAST		Drei Nächte, bitte.
EMPFANGSDAME	2	Wir haben zur Zeit leider keine Doppelzimmer *mit Bad* frei. Wir haben sehr viele Gäste. Aber ich könnte Ihnen ein Doppelzimmer *mit Dusche* anbieten.
• GAST		Ja, das ist mir auch recht.
EMPFANGSDAME		Sechzig Mark pro Übernachtung kostet das Doppelzimmer.
• GAST		Pro Person?
EMPFANGSDAME		Nein, mein Herr! Sechzig Mark, das ist der Preis für zwei Personen.
• GAST	3	Gut, das ist in Ordnung. Ist in dem *Preis das Frühstück* enthalten?
EMPFANGSDAME		Selbstverständlich, mein Herr.
• GAST		Gut. Ich nehme das Doppelzimmer mit Dusche.
EMPFANGSDAME		Es ist Zimmer sechsundsiebzig, vierter Stock. Hier ist Ihr Schlüssel!
• GAST		Wo ist der Lift? Unser Gepäck ist sehr schwer.

EMPFANGSDAME	Rechts vom Haupteingang. Ich rufe Ihnen aber einen Hotel-Boy. Franz! Hilf bitte dem Herrn von Zimmer sechsundsiebzig.
• GAST	Das Gepäck ist draußen im Auto. Ich gehe und hole es.
• EMPFANGSDAME	Franz wird Ihnen helfen, mein Herr. Oh, einen Augenblick noch. Wann möchten Sie das Frühstück einnehmen?
• GAST	Wird es auch auf dem Zimmer serviert?
EMPFANGSDAME	Ja, mein Herr, oder auch unten im Speisesaal, ganz nach Ihrem Wunsch.
• GAST	Bitte servieren Sie es uns um neun Uhr auf dem Zimmer.
EMPFANGSDAME	Ist in Ordnung, mein Herr. Und was wünschen Sie zu trinken, Kaffee, Tee oder Schokolade?
• GAST	Kaffee mit Milch für mich und Tee ohne Milch für meine Frau.
EMPFANGSDAME	Ist in Ordnung. Ich habe es notiert. Ich wünsche Ihnen einen angenehmen Aufenthalt in unserem Hotel.
• GAST	Franz, sind Sie bitte so nett und nehmen Sie die beiden großen Koffer, ich nehme dann das andere Gepäck.
FRANZ	Jawohl. Bitte folgen Sie mir zum Aufzug. Ihr Zimmer liegt im vierten Stock.
• GAST	Ist dies der einzige Aufzug im Hotel?

8

FRANZ	Nein, mein Herr. Wenn Sie in das Restaurant oder in die Bar wollen, nehmen Sie den Aufzug am Ende der Flure. Er führt genau in das Restaurant. So, hier ist Zimmer sechsundsiebzig. Bitte sehr. Ich wünsche Ihnen schöne Tage.
• GAST	Recht herzlichen Dank. Und das ist für Sie.
FRANZ	Vielen Dank.

Fußnote
1 In Deutschland unterscheidet man Einzelzimmer, Doppelzimmer und häufig auch für Familien ein Doppelzimmer mit einer oder zwei weiteren Schlafmöglichkeiten.
2 Die Mehrzahl deutscher Hotelzimmer ist mit Bad/WC oder Dusche/WC ausgestattet.
3 Der Übernachtungspreis gilt immer inclusive Frühstück, das in der Regel im Speisesaal eingenommen wird.

Notes
1 In Germany hotel bedrooms may be classified as single, double or (for families) double with one or two additional beds.
2 Most hotel bedrooms will have either a bath and WC or a shower and WC.
3 The price for one night always includes breakfast, which is usually eaten in the dining room.

Im Cafe[1]

• GAST	Herr Ober!
OBER	Ja bitte?

• GAST 2 Ich hätte gerne ein *Kännchen Kaffee* mit Milch und Kuchen. Was für Sorten haben Sie?

OBER 3 Dort ist ein *Buffet*. Bitte gehen Sie dorthin und suchen Sie sich etwas aus. Sie bekommen dann einen Bon, den geben Sie mir, und ich bringe Ihnen Ihren Kuchen.

• GAST Danke sehr.

. . . .

OBER 4 *Haben Sie sich etwas ausgesucht?*

• GAST Ja, hier ist mein Bon.

OBER Ihr Kuchen kommt sofort.

. . . .

OBER So, hier ist Ihr Kännchen Kaffee und ein Stück Erdbeerkuchen mit Sahne.

• GAST Können Sie mir bitte noch ein Päckchen Zigaretten bringen?

OBER Ja, welche Sorte darf es sein?

• GAST Bringen Sie mir bitte zwanzig Rothmans und die Rechnung bitte.

. . . .

OBER	Sie hatten ein Kännchen Kaffee für drei Mark, ein Stück Erdbeerkuchen mit Sahne zwei Mark fünfzig, ein Päckchen Zigaretten drei Mark. Macht zusammen acht Mark fünfzig.
• GAST	Ist die Bedienung inbegriffen?
OBER	Ja, vielen Dank.

An der Verkaufstheke

VERKÄUFERIN	Sie wünschen, bitte?
• KUNDIN	Was haben Sie hier für leckere Kekse?
VERKÄUFERIN	Das sind Mandelkekse. Hundert fünfundzwanzig Gramm kosten zwei Mark.
• KUNDIN	Oh, dann geben Sie mir bitte zweihundertfünfzig Gramm.
VERKÄUFERIN	Hier bitte schön. Sonst noch etwas?
• KUNDIN	Ja. Ich hätte gern noch eine Schachtel Pralinen. Haben Sie Pralinen, die mit Cognac gefüllt sind?
VERKÄUFERIN	Ja, diese hier. Sie kosten acht Mark fünfzig.
• KUNDIN	Bitte packen Sie mir die Pralinen als Geschenk ein. Hier sind die zwölf Mark fünfzig.
VERKÄUFERIN	Hier sind die Kekse und die Pralinen. Vielen Dank und auf Wiedersehen.
• KUNDIN	Auf Wiedersehen!

Fußnote

1   In manchen Gegenden nennt man das Café "Konditorei". Am häufigsten ist das deutsche Café einer Bäckerei oder Konditorei unmittelbar angeschlossen. Es dient fast ausschließlich dem Verzehr von Kaffee, Tee und Kuchen.

2   In Ausflugslokalen können Sie fast immer nur Kännchen Kaffee bekommen. In den Stadtcafés wird der Kaffee aber auch tassenweise serviert. Tee wird immer in Teegläsern serviert, man muß jedoch bei Tee den Zusatz "mit Milch" dem Ober sagen, da der Deutsche den Tee mit Zitrone bevorzugt.

3   Man sucht sich den Kuchen am Buffet selbst aus. Das Angebot ist immer sehr vielfältig und besteht zur Hauptsache aus: Obsttorten, frischen Sahnetorten verfeinert mit Schokolade, Nüssen, Kirschen oder Likören und Buttercremetorten.

4   Städtische Cafés haben in ihrem Angebot oftmals eine begrenzte Anzahl von Gerichten wie Pasteten, Toast mit Schinken oder Fleisch oder verschiedene Suppen.

Notes

1   In some parts of Germany a cafe is called "Konditorei". Most cafes are part of a baker's shop; you can buy coffee or tea, and different sorts of cakes.

2   In tourist centres coffee is served in small pots, but in most cafes in towns you'll get a cup of coffee. Tea is always served in special tea-glasses. If you order tea, you must say "with milk" because Germans prefer tea with lemon.

3   You choose the cakes you want from the counter, where there is always a great variety: fruit tarts, fresh cream cakes, maybe with nuts, chocolate, cherries or a liqueur, and buttercream gâteaux.

4   Cafes in towns sometimes offer a few small snacks on their menu, such as pies or pasties, toast with ham or some other meat, or various soups.

Auf der Bank

• MR. SMITH	1	Guten Tag. *Kann ich bei Ihnen Geld einwechseln*?
ANGESTELLTE		Nein, bei mir nicht, aber meine Kollegin dort drüben kann Ihnen weiterhelfen.
• MR. SMITH		Guten Tag. Ich möchte Geld einwechseln.
ANGESTELLTE	2	Haben Sie *Bargeld, Euro-Schecks* oder *Traveller-Schecks*?
• MR. SMITH		Traveller-Schecks. Hier sind zwei Schecks im Wert von je fünfzig Pfund. Geben Sie ˜ mir bitte Deutsche Mark dafür.
ANGESTELLTE		Einen Moment, ich sehe nur nach, wie der Tageskurs lautet.
		Sie bekommen für ein Englisches Pfund vier Mark fünf.
• MR. SMITH		In Ordnung, hier sind sie.
ANGESTELLTE		Unterschreiben Sie bitte die Schecks an dieser Stelle. So, Sie bekommen für Ihre Schecks vierhundertfünf Mark.
• MR. SMITH		Geben Sie mir das Geld in kleinen Scheinen.
ANGESTELLTE		Ist es so recht?
• MR. SMITH		Ja, aber geben Sie mir für diesen zehn Mark-Schein Münzen, damit ich telefonieren kann. Vielen Dank. Auf Wiedersehen!

Fußnote

1   Deutschland hat neben seinen Banken auch noch die örtlichen Sparkassen, bei denen man zu den Öffnungszeiten ebenfalls ausländisches Geld wechseln kann. In der Regel öffnen die Banken an Werktagen um 9.00 Uhr und schließen um 16.00 Uhr. Außer auf großen Bahnhöfen und Flughäfen gibt es keine privaten Wechselstuben.

2   Die verschiedenen Zahlungsmittel (Bargeld, Schecks, Traveller-Schecks) haben unterschiedliche Tageskurse, wobei im Einzelnen keine Empfehlung über das geeignetste Zahlungsmittel gegeben werden kann.

Notes

1   Besides the usual German banks you'll find a lot of local "Savings Banks" ("*Sparkassen*") run by the local authorities, where you can change your money. Banks in general are usually open from 9 a.m. to 4 p.m. on weekdays. Some may open on Saturday mornings. There are no private foreign exchange bureaux other than on big railway stations and airports.

2   Cheques, banknotes and travellers' cheques all have different exchange rates, but nobody can say which one is the highest at any particular time.

Beim Bäcker

BÄCKER	Guten Morgen Frau Müller.
• KUNDIN	Guten Morgen Herr Meier.
BÄCKER	Was darf es sein?
• KUNDIN	1 Zehn frische *Brötchen*, bitte.
BÄCKER	Hier bitte die Brötchen sind ganz frisch, nicht aus der Kühltruhe. Sonst noch etwas?
• KUNDIN	2 Warten Sie! Ach ja, ein Pfund *Schwarzbrot*, aber dünne Scheiben und 3 ein halbes Pfund *Butter*. Ich denke, das ist dann alles. Ach so, was haben Sie denn diese Woche im Sonderangebot?
BÄCKER	4 Hier haben wir eine neue *Kaffeesorte*, nur sieben Mark fünfundneunzig das Pfund.
• KUNDIN	Ist er gut?
BÄCKER	Nun, ich habe ihn selbst noch nicht probiert. Sie wissen, meine Frau liebt ihre Sorte über alles.
• KUNDIN	Dann laß ich es auch. Ich muß sowieso mit dem Geld sparsam umgehen. Es ist erst der fünfundzwanzigste, und ich habe nicht mehr viel. Was macht das zusammen?
BÄCKER	Die Brötchen kosten zwei Mark, zwanzig Pfennig das Stück, das Schwarzbrot kostet eine Mark neunundsechzig und die Butter eine Mark neunundachtzig. Warten Sie, das macht insgesamt fünf Mark achtundfünfzig.
• KUNDIN	Hier sind sechs Mark.

BÄCKER	Zweiundvierzig Pfennig zurück. Vielen Dank, Frau Müller.
	Auf Wiedersehen.
• KUNDIN	Auf Wiedersehen, Herr Meier.

Fußnote

1 In den verschiedenen Landschaften Deutschlands haben die Brötchen ein unterschiedliches Aussehen und andere Namen. "Brötchen" kann dennoch als allgemein verständlich angesehen werden.

2 Viele Bäckereien haben sich auf das Backen von verschiedenen Brotsorten spezialisiert. So kann der Käufer oftmals zwischen 10-15 Brotsorten wählen.

3 Bäckereien haben auch am Sonntag für 1 bis 2 Stunden geöffnet. Aus diesem Grund führen auch viele ein geringes Angebot an anderen Grundnahrungsmitteln wie Butter, Wurst und Milch.

4 Viele Bäckereien haben sich einer der Großröstereien für Kaffee angeschlossen und betreuen ein Kaffeedepot.

Notes

1 In some parts of Germany fresh rolls *(Brötchen)* have different names—and look different as well. But if you ask for *Brötchen* everyone knows what you want.

2 Many bakers specialise in baking different sorts of bread. Sometimes you may choose between ten and fifteen types of loaf.

3 Bakers also open on Sundays for one or two hours. That is why they have a small supply of other basic foodstuffs such as butter, sausages and milk.

4 Many bakers have a contract with one of the big coffee firms and offer an assortment of coffees.

Auf dem Bahnhof

Am Fahrkartenschalter

• MARTIN		Guten Tag. Ich hätte gerne eine Fahrkarte nach Köln.
SCHALTERBEAMTE		Erste oder zweite Klasse?
• MARTIN	1, 2	Zweite Klasse bitte. *Können Sie mir sagen*, wann der nächste *Zug* geht? Ich muß um zwölf Uhr in Köln sein, da meine Freunde aus London um zwölf Uhr dreißig am Kölner Hauptbahnhof eintreffen.
SCHALTERBEAMTE		Der nächste Zug geht um elf Uhr acht. Da haben Sie genug Zeit, um pünktlich in Köln zu sein.
• MARTIN		An welchem Bahnsteig fährt mein Zug ab?
SCHALTERBEAMTE		Bahnsteig 2. Hier ist Ihre Karte.
• MARTIN		**Vielen Dank!**

Am Hauptbahnhof

• MARTIN	3	Können Sie mir bitte sagen, *auf welchem Bahnsteig* der Zug aus Ostende, der um zwölf Uhr dreißig eintrifft, ankommt?

AUSKUNFT	Einen Moment. Ja, der Zug kommt auf Bahnsteig 7a/b an. Aber es ist gemeldet, daß er zehn Minuten Verspätung hat.
• MARTIN	Das macht nichts, dann werde ich mir noch eine Zeitung kaufen.

Am Kiosk

• MARTIN	4 Guten Tag. Haben Sie *ausländische Zeitungen*?
VERKÄUFERIN	Aber ja! Was möchten Sie? Französische, englische, türkische, spanische, italienische, holländische oder dänische?
• MARTIN	Ich möchte eine englische Zeitung.
VERKÄUFERIN	Hm, da hätte ich Daily Express, Daily Mail, Financial Times oder Daily Mirror anzubieten.
• MARTIN	Geben Sie mir bitte den Daily Express, und können Sie mir sagen, wo der Bahnsteig 7a/b ist?
VERKÄUFERIN	Dort entlang und dann an der Telefonzelle rechts. Da werden Sie das Schild 7a/b an der linken Wand finden.
• MARTIN	Vielen Dank! Oh, der Lautsprecher sagt den Zug gerade an, ich muß mich beeilen. Auf Wiedersehen!

Auf dem Bahnsteig

- MARTIN — Hallo Stephanie, hallo Peter!
  PETER & STEPHANIE — Hallo Martin!

- MARTIN — Ich freue mich, Euch wiederzusehen. Habt Ihr eine angenehme Reise gehabt?

  PETER — Ja danke. Die Bahnfahrt war sehr interessant. Aber es dauerte doch sehr lange.

- MARTIN — Und wie war die Kanalüberfahrt, Stephanie?

  STEPHANIE — Es war herrlich, Martin. Die Sonne ging auf und wir hatten eine ruhige See.

- MARTIN — So, dann wollen wir mal nach Hause fahren. Habt Ihr Euer Gepäck?

  STEPHANIE — Ja, es ist alles klar.

Fußnote

1 Große Bahnhöfe haben ein spezielles Auskunftsbüro. Kurzinformationen erhält man aber auch am Fahrkartenschalter.

2 Im deutschen Schienennetz verkehren:
Nahverkehrszüge, Eilzüge, D-Züge, Inter-City Züge und TEE-Züge. Für Inter-City Züge und TEE-Züge muß jedoch ein Sonderzuschlag gezahlt werden.

3 Man braucht heute keine Bahnsteigkarte mehr, will man jemanden vom Zug abholen. Im D-Zug-, Inter-City- und TEE-Zugverkehr geben Wagenstandanzeiger den genauen Haltepunkt der einzelnen Eisenbahnwaggons an. Diese Wagenstandanzeiger befinden sich auf den Bahnsteigen.

4 Aktuelle britische Tageszeitungen bekommt man jedoch nur in den deutschen Großstädten und dann meistens an den Bahnhofskiosken oder in Buchhandlungen.

Notes

1   The larger railway stations have an information office, while simple enquiries can be answered by the assistant at the ticket office.

2   German trains are classified as: *Nahverkehrszüge, Eilzüge, D-Züge, Inter-City Züge* and *TEE-Züge* (Trans European Express). For travel on Inter-City and TEE trains you must pay an extra charge.

3   You don't need a platform ticket in order to meet somebody. On the platform itself you will find timetables and lists which tell you the number of every coach, and whereabouts down the platform any particular coach will stop (this applies to D-Zug, Inter-City and TEE).

4   British newspapers are obtainable only in the larger German cities, at station kiosks or in bookshops.

Auf der Post[1]

SCHALTERBEAMTER	Ja, bitte?
● KUNDIN	Ich möchte gern eine Briefmarke für diese Ansichtskarte nach England. Wieviel kostet es?
SCHALTERBEAMTER	Es kostet sechzig Pfennig.
● KUNDIN	Und wie teuer ist ein Brief nach England?
SCHALTERBEAMTER	Nach England kostet ein Brief achtzig Pfennig. In die anderen EG-Staaten sechzig Pfennig, außer Irland und Dänemark.
● KUNDIN	Tatsächlich? Dann geben Sie mir bitte eine sechzig Pfennig- und eine achtzig Pfennig-Briefmarke.
SCHALTERBEAMTER	Sonst noch ein Wunsch, meine Dame?
● KUNDIN	2 Oh ja, beinahe hätte ich es vergessen. *Ich möchte gern London anrufen.* Kann ich dies von hier aus tun?
SCHALTERBEAMTER	Ja, geben Sie mir die Telefonnummer und gehen Sie in Telefonkabine 3. Wenn es klingelt, nehmen Sie bitte den Telefonhörer ab. Nach Beendigung des Gesprächs zahlen Sie die Kosten hier bei mir am Schalter.

• KUNDIN	Wie teuer ist ein drei Minuten-Gespräch?
SCHALTERBEAMTER	Eine Minute kostet etwa zwei Mark dreißig.
• KUNDIN	Es hat sich leider niemand gemeldet. Ich versuche es noch einmal in einer Stunde.
SCHALTERBEAMTER	3 Dann haben wir aber schon geschlossen. *Sie können jedoch auch von der Telefonzelle aus nach England anrufen.*
• KUNDIN	Das ist fein. Können Sie mir die Vorwahl geben?
SCHALTERBEAMTER	Sie wählen null null vier vier (0044) für England; dann die Vorwahl der Stadt. Hier lassen sie bitte die null (0) zu Beginn der Vorwahl weg; dann folgt die Nummer für den Privatanschluss.
• KUNDIN	Vielen Dank und auf Wiedersehen.

Fußnote

1 Die deutschen Postämter haben wie folgt geöffnet: Montags-Freitags . . 8.00-12.00, 15.00-18.00. Samstags . . 8.00-12.00. Die Öffnungszeiten sind auch an den einzelnen Postämtern angeschlagen.

2 In allen Postämtern kann man vom Schalter aus telefonieren. Dazu stehen Telefonkabinen zur Verfügung. Außerdem liegen Telefonverzeichnisse der gesamten Bundesrepublik am Schalter aus.

3 In Deutschland ist das gesamte Telefonnetz automatisiert. Deshalb gibt es keine Handvermittlung mehr. Bei Fragen können Sie die Auskunft 118 oder 0118 wählen.

Notes

1   German post office opening hours are: Monday-Friday . . 8.00 a.m.-12 noon, 3.00 p.m.-6.00 p.m. Saturday . . 8.00 a.m.-12 noon. These opening hours are displayed on every post office door or window.

2   You can make a telephone call from any post office in Germany. Kiosks are situated inside the building, and directories for all districts in the Federal Republic are available.

3   Germany has an automatic telephone system, and there is no longer any service via an operator. If you have any questions, dial 118 or 0118 and the *Auskunft* ("Information") will help you.

Im Schuhgeschäft

VERKÄUFERIN 1 Guten Tag, mein Herr. *Was kann ich fur Sie tun?*

● KUNDE Ich hätte gerne ein Paar bequeme Schuhe, aber nicht so teuer.

VERKÄUFERIN Ja, schauen Sie bitte mal in diesen Regalen nach. Vielleicht gefällt Ihnen ein Schuh. Welche Größe brauchen Sie?

● KUNDE 2 *Dreiundvierzig.*

VERKÄUFERIN Hier sind die Regale mit Schuhen Größe dreiundvierzig. Sollte Ihnen nichts gefallen, dann zeige ich Ihnen noch andere. Nehmen Sie bitte Platz. Ich werde Ihnen jetzt verschiedene andere Exemplare vorführen. Hier habe ich ein schönes Paar mit Gummisohle, jedoch nur in Schwarz.

● KUNDE Oh ja, der sitzt gut. Darf ich den linken Schuh auch anprobieren? Wie teuer sind sie?

VERKÄUFERIN Hier haben Sie auch den linken Schuh. Sie kosten achtundneunzig Mark.

● KUNDE Das ist ja teuer, aber sie gefallen mir. Ich nehme sie.

VERKÄUFERIN Kommen Sie bitte mit zur Kasse. Benötigen Sie eine spezielle Schuhcreme?

● KUNDE Nein danke. Ich habe noch Schuhcreme zu Hause.

VERKÄUFERIN	Achtundneunzig Mark bitte!
KUNDE	Hier sind hundert Mark.
VERKÄUFERIN	Und hier sind zwei Mark zurück. Auf Wiedersehen und vielen Dank.

(• precedes KUNDE)

Fußnote

1 Die meisten deutschen Schuhgeschäfte sind zum System der Selbstbedienung übergegangen. In den Regalen liegt jeweils der rechte Schuh aus, er kann anprobiert werden, während beim tatsächlichem Kauf der linke dann von der Verkäuferin geholt wird.

2 Die Schuhgrößen in Deutschland entsprechen den englischen Schuhgrößen wie folgt:

deutsch:	35	36	37	38	39	40	41	42	43	44	45	46
englisch:	3	$3\frac{1}{2}$	4	5	6	$6\frac{1}{2}$	7	8	9	$9\frac{1}{2}$	$10\frac{1}{2}$	11

Notes

1 Most German shoe-shops have started self-service. You'll find the right-hand shoe on the shelves; you can try it on and the left one is fetched by the shop assistant if you think you will buy them.

2 Shoe sizes in Germany are different to those in Britain—as shown in the table above.

Beim Fleischer[1]

- KUNDIN   Guten Tag!

  FLEISCHER   2   Guten Tag, *was darf es sein?*

- KUNDIN   3   Ich hätte gerne *1 ½ Pfund* Gulasch.

  FLEISCHER   Rindfleisch oder Schweinefleisch?

- KUNDIN   4   Bitte von beidem, halb und halb. Und dann geben Sie mir bitte noch vier *Koteletts.*

  FLEISCHER   Darf es noch etwas sein?

- KUNDIN   5   Ja, ich brauche noch *Aufschnitt.* Ein Viertel Pfund Leberwurst, ein Viertel Pfund Salami und ein halbes Pfund gekochten Schinken.

  FLEISCHER   Hätten Sie sonst noch einen Wunsch?

- KUNDIN   Ich hätte gern noch Fleisch zum Grillen. Können Sie mir da etwas empfehlen?

  FLEISCHER   Ja, ich habe hier sehr leckere Grill-Bratwürstchen und dann natürlich auch Steaks.

- KUNDIN   Dann geben Sie mir bitte zehn Bratwürste und fünf Steaks.

  FLEISCHER   Sonst noch etwas?

- KUNDIN   Nein, vielen Dank, das wäre alles.

  FLEISCHER   Das macht zweiundvierzig Mark zwanzig, meine Dame.

- KUNDIN   Hier sind fünfzig Mark.

| FLEISCHER | Und hier ist Ihr Wechselgeld, sieben Mark achtzig. Herzlichen Dank und auf Wiedersehen. |
| • KUNDIN | Auf Wiedersehen. |

Fußnote

1 In verschiedenen Regionen heißt der Fleischer auch Metzger.
2 Der deutsche Käufer kennt zwar das Anstellen, praktiziert es jedoch in den wenigsten Fällen. Jeder Einzelne paßt auf, wer vor ihm da war und meldet sich dann, wenn der Verkäufer fragt "Der Nächste, bitte?".
3 Das deutsche Pfund sind 500 Gramm.
4 Es gibt zwei Sorten von Kotelett; Nackenkotelett und Lummerkotelett.
5 Unter Aufschnitt wird eine Mischung von verschiedenen Wurstsorten zu einem gemeinsamen Preis verstanden.

Notes

1 In some parts of Germany the butcher is called *Metzger*, not *Fleischer*.
2 The German customer knows a lot about queuing up, but this doesn't happen very often. Instead, everyone knows when his or her turn should be, and responds when the shop-assistant calls out "Who's next?".
3 The German *Pfund* or pound is 500g.
4 You can get two sorts of cutlets; neck and boned cutlets.
5 *Aufschnitt* means that you get four or five different sorts of sausage for one price.

In der Apotheke[1] und beim Zahnarzt

In der Apotheke

• KUNDE		Guten Tag!
APOTHEKERIN	2	Guten Tag! *Womit kann ich Ihnen helfen?*
• KUNDE		Meine Frau hat furchtbare Zahnschmerzen. Was können wir dagegen tun?
APOTHEKERIN	3	Ich gebe Ihnen eine Packung Schmerztabletten mit. Davon soll sie jetzt eine Tablette und nach vier Stunden eine weitere nehmen. Sollten sich die Schmerzen nicht bessern, müßte sie *einen Zahnarzt aufsuchen.*
• KUNDE		Können Sie mir bitte sagen, welcher Zahnarzt zu erreichen ist?
APOTHEKERIN	4	Ja, ich gebe Ihnen ein Verzeichnis über *die Zahnärzte, die dienstbereit sind.*
• KUNDE		Was muß ich zahlen?
APOTHEKERIN		Die Tabletten kosten fünf Mark fünfundzwanzig.
• KUNDE		Vielen Dank. Auf Wiedersehen!
APOTHEKERIN		Auf Wiedersehen!

Beim Zahnarzt

ARZTHELFERIN	Frau Smith kommen Sie bitte?
ZAHNARZT	Guten Morgen Frau Smith. Wie kann ich Ihnen helfen?
• MRS. SMITH	Ich habe heftige Zahnschmerzen. Gestern abend ist mir eine Füllung herausgefallen.
ZAHNARZT	Lehnen Sie den Kopf bitten hinten an. Können Sie den Mund ein wenig mehr öffnen?
• MRS. SMITH	Rechts der zweite Backenzahn oben.
ZAHNARZT	Ist es dieser?
• MRS. SMITH	Ja, der, den Sie gerade berührt haben.
ZAHNARZT	Ich glaube, es wird Ihnen ein wenig Schmerzen bereiten. Es ist gerade eine empfindliche Stelle, aber ich bin gleich mit dem Bohrer fertig. Jetzt ist es gut. Die neue Füllung kann hinein. Würden Sie bitte den Mund ausspülen.
• MRS. SMITH	Ich fühle mich schon besser.
ZAHNARZT	Bitte essen Sie nichts in den nächsten drei Stunden. Ich schaue mir noch schnell die anderen Zähne an. Hier ist einer, der Ihnen bald Ärger machen wird. Wenn Sie wieder zu Hause sind, gehen Sie schnell zu Ihrem Zahnarzt.
• MRS. SMITH	Ja, das werde ich auch tun. Vielen Dank.

| ZAHNARZT | Auf Wiedersehen Frau Smith. |
| • MRS. SMITH | Auf Wiedersehen Herr Doktor. |

Am Nachmittag in der Apotheke

APOTHEKERIN	Guten Tag! Sind die Zahnschmerzen besser geworden?
• KUNDE	Nein, wir mußten den Zahnarzt aufsuchen. Er hat den Zahn gefüllt und mir ein Rezept mitgegeben.
APOTHEKERIN	5 Ja, ich sehe, ein stärkeres Mittel gegen Schmerzen und ein Mittel, um einer Wundinfizierung vorzubeugen. *Sie können solche Medikamente auch nur auf Rezept bekommen.*
	So, hier sind Ihre Medikamente. Das macht zweiundzwanzig Mark fünfzig. Haben Sie noch einen Wunsch?
• KUNDE	Ja, ich habe vorhin festgestellt, daß meine Tabletten, die ich regelmäßig einnehmen muß, alle sind. Es sind Tabletten gegen zu hohen Blutdruck.
APOTHEKERIN	Können Sie mir den Namen des Mittels sagen?
• KUNDE	Ja, hier ist die leere Packung.
APOTHEKERIN	Das ist ein ausländisches Präparat, das unter diesem Namen in Deutschland nicht vertrieben wird. Aber ich kann Ihnen mit einem deutschen

	Medikament helfen. Es hat die gleichen Wirkstoffe wie Ihr Medikament, nur einen anderen Namen.
• KUNDE	Damit wäre mir sehr geholfen. Was habe ich zu zahlen?
APOTHEKERIN	Ich bekomme dafür sieben Mark fünfundsiebzig. Das macht insgesamt dreißig Mark fünfundzwanzig.
• KUNDE	Vielen Dank für Ihre Hilfe, auf Wiedersehen.
APOTHEKERIN	Auf Wiedersehen und gute Besserung für Ihre Frau!

Fußnote

1   Im Gegensatz zu Großbritannien sind in Deutschland alle Apotheken selbständige private Unternehmen und z.B. keiner Drogerienkette wie "Boots" angeschlossen. Sie heißen Apotheke und führen ausschließlich Medikamente und ein kleines Sortiment Drogerieartikel jedoch unter medizinischem Aspekt.

2   In jeder Stadt in Deutschland besteht nach Ladenschlußzeit und an den Wochenenden ein Notdienst. Welche Apotheke Notdienst hat, kann in der Lokalzeitung nachgelesen werden. Es ist aber auch durch Aushang an jeder Apotheke einsehbar. "Dienstbereit" heißt Notdienst. Der Apotheker wird durch eine Klingel zur Tür gerufen (nachts).

3   Deutsche Zahnärzte haben lange Wartezeiten. Machen Sie Ihren Fall dringend, damit eine Behandlung noch am gleichen Tag erfolgt.

4   An Wochenenden hat jeweils ein Zahnarzt in der Stadt Notdienst. Welcher Zahnarzt das ist, erfahren Sie aus der Zeitung oder durch eine Telefonansage. Auch in den dienstbereiten Apotheken können Sie die Anschrift erfahren.

5   In Deutschland wird ebenfalls in zwei Kategorien von Medikamenten unterschieden. Rezeptfreie und solche, die nur durch die Verordnung des Arztes in der Apotheke zu erhalten sind.

Notes

1 In Germany all chemists' shops are independent private concerns. There are no chainstore chemists like Boots in Britain. They are called "Apotheke" and sell exclusively medicines and a small assortment of drugstore goods which have some medicinal use.

2 In every town you will find an *Apotheke* that is open all night or over the weekend. Those that are closed will display a notice showing which one is open, and the local newspaper also advertises the *"dienstbereit"* or "duty" chemist. The owner or an assistant pharmacist opens the door after you've rung the night bell.

3 German dentists have long waiting-lists. Make out an urgent case for yourself, so that you will get treatment on the same day.

4 At weekends only one dentist in each town is on duty. The local newspaper will show his name, or you can call a special phone number to find out who it is. The chemist can also help you locate the address.

5 In Germany there are two categories of medicines; those sold over the counter and those which can only be obtained on a doctor's prescription.

Eine Stadtrundfahrt durch Köln

Im Fremdenverkehrsbüro

ANGESTELLTER	Guten Tag. Sie wünschen bitte?
• TOURIST	1 *Ich möchte gern eine Stadtrundfahrt buchen.*
ANGESTELLTER	Ja gern. Sie beginnt in einer Stunde und der Bus fährt am Busbahnhof dort vorne ab.
• TOURIST	Wie teuer ist die Stadtrundfahrt?
ANGESTELLTER	Zehn Mark bitte.
	(Der Tourist hat neben anderen Touristen im Bus Platz genommen.)
STADTFÜHRER	Guten Morgen, meine Damen und Herren! Mein Name ist Gerd Radandt. Ich möchte Ihnen in den nächsten zwei Stunden unsere schöne Stadt Köln zeigen. Wenn Sie während der Fahrt Fragen haben, werde ich sie Ihnen gern beantworten.
	(Der Bus setzt sich in Bewegung.)
STADTFÜHRER	Meine Damen und Herren, während wir jetzt ein Stück am Rhein entlang fahren, werde ich Ihnen etwas über Köln, eine der ältesten Städte Deutschlands erzählen. Köln wurde bereits von den Römern vor Christi Geburt

als Stützpunkt am Rhein gegründet, wurde unter Kaiser Claudius fünfzig nach Christo zum Mittelpunkt des römischen Germaniens und erhielt den Namen Colonia Agrippinensis.

- TOURIST

Gibt es heute noch Zeugen aus dieser römischen Vergangenheit?

STADTFÜHRER

Ja. In den letzten Jahrzehnten entdeckte man eine Vielzahl von Bauwerken römischen Ursprungs. Das Gelände um den Dom herum war früher eine römische Siedlung und viele Fundamente und Mauern sind noch erhalten. Ebenso Mosaike, Säulen, Türme und viele andere Gegenstände.

Eine umfangreiche Sammlung zeigt das neben dem Dom liegende Römisch-Germanische Museum.

- TOURIST

2 *Hat Köln noch andere wichtige berühmte Museen?*

STADTFÜHRER

Ja, es gibt einige Museen und auch ein Völkerkundemuseum.

Hier rechts sehen Sie jetzt die Altstadt Kölns. Die schönen Häuserfassaden stammen aus dem Mittelalter. Die Altstadt ist mit ihren vielen Restaurants und Bierlokalen ein beliebter Treffpunkt. Hier auf dem "Alten Markt" findet jedes Jahr im Februar zur Karnevalszeit die Eröffnung des Kölner Straßenkarnevals statt.

• TOURIST	3 *Findet nicht auch immer ein großer Karnevalszug statt?*
STADTFÜHRER	Das ist richtig. Am Rosenmontag, dem Höhepunkt des rheinischen Karnevals gibt es einen Umzug durch die Straßen Kölns, der fünf bis sechs Kilometer lang ist.
	Wir biegen jetzt auf einen der Kölner Ringe ein. Er ist die mittelalterliche Begrenzung Kölns. Sie können hier noch viele Stadttore aus dieser Zeit sehen. Vom Ring führen fast alle Straßen in Richtung Stadtmitte auf den Dom zu.
• TOURIST	Was ist das dort hinten für ein Turm?
STADTFÜHRER	4 Das ist der neue Postturm der erst kürzlich gebaut wurde und von den Kölnern "Colonius" genannt wird.
	Wir fahren nun in Richtung Innenstadt durch das Bankenviertel zum *Kölner Dom.* Er ist das größte gotische Bauwerk auf deutschem Boden. Der Baubeginn lag im Jahre 1248 (zwölfhundertachtundvierzig) und vollendet wurde der Dom erst im Jahre 1880 (achtzehnhundertachtzig).
• TOURIST	Können Sie uns einen Tip geben, wo wir hier einkaufen können?

STADTFÜHRER	Direkt vom Dom geht eine der beiden großen Einkaufsstraßen die "Hohe Straße" ab und trifft am Ende auf die "Schildergasse", die andere große Einkaufsstraße. Zu Beginn der "Hohen Straße" können Sie den "Heinzelmännchen-Brunnen" sehen, der auf Grund einer alten Kölner Sage gebaut wurde.
	Wir kommen nun wieder zum Ausgangspunkt unserer Fahrt zurück. Dort vorne ist schon der Rhein.
• TOURIST	5 Auf dem Rhein sieht man sehr viele Ausflugsboote. *Bis wohin kann man damit fahren*?
STADTFÜHRER	Es gibt im Sommer einen regelmäßigen Schiffsverkehr zwischen Köln und den rheinaufwärts gelegenen Städten Bonn, Königswinter und Koblenz. Sie können aber auch an einer der abendlichen Tanzpartys auf einem Dampfer teilnehmen. Ich hoffe die Stadtrundfahrt hat Ihnen Freude gemacht und ich wünsche Ihnen einen angenehmen Aufenthalt in unserer Domstadt.
	Auf Wiedersehen.

Fußnote

1 Eine Stadtrundfahrt kann man im Fremdenverkehrsbüro der Stadt Köln am Dom buchen.
2 Die Kölner Museen haben bestimmte Öffnungszeiten. Es ist anzuraten, sich vorher zu erkundigen, ob das Museum geöffnet ist.
3 Der Kölner Karneval beginnt immer nach Neujahr und dauert bis Aschermittwoch. Höhepunkt sind die letzten fünf Tage vor Aschermittwoch mit dem großen Umzug am Rosenmontag.
4 Man kann den rechten Turm des Kölner Domes besteigen. Über fünfhundert Stufen führen bis in die Turmspitze. Der Eingang ist rechts vom Hauptportal.
5 Ein schöner Ausflug auf dem Rhein führt von Köln nach Königswinter und zurück. Hier in Königswinter kann man dann eine Wanderung durch das Siebengebirge machen.

Notes

1 You can book a sightseeing tour at the tourist office near Cologne cathedral.
2 The museums of Cologne are not open every day. It is advisable to ask first if they are open.
3 Cologne carnival starts after New Year's Day and lasts until Ash Wednesday. The last five days before Ash Wednesday form the climax, with a great procession on Rose Monday (just before Shrove Tuesday).
4 You can climb the right-hand tower of Cologne cathedral. More than 500 steps take you right up to the top of the tower. The entrance is on the right, inside the main door.
5 There is a pleasant trip on the Rhine from Cologne to Königswinter (Bonn) and back again. At Königswinter you can walk in the "Seven Hills" (*Siebengebirge*).

Auf der Polizei[1]

POLIZEIBEAMTER		Ja bitte, Sie wünschen?
• MR. RUSTON	2	*Bitte können Sie mir helfen*, ich habe meinen Paß verloren.
POLIZEIBEAMTER		Kommen Sie bitte hier in diesen Raum. Nehmen Sie bitte Platz und beantworten Sie mir folgende Fragen! Wie heißen Sie?
• MR. RUSTON		Michael Ruston.
POLIZEIBEAMTER		Wo wohnen Sie?
• MR. RUSTON		In London, Edenhill Road Nummer 281.
POLIZEIBEAMTER		Wann sind Sie geboren und wo?
• MR. RUSTON		Am 1.6.1948 in Southampton.
POLIZEIBEAMTER		Unterschreiben Sie bitte diese Verlusterklärung hier.
• MR. RUSTON		So, und was muß ich nun machen?
POLIZEIBEAMTER		Ich gebe Ihnen die Adresse des Britischen Konsulates in Düsseldorf und dorthin müssen Sie gehen und diese Verlusterklärung vorzeigen. Sie bekommen dann einen vorläufigen Paß ausgestellt.
• MR. RUSTON		Ich danke Ihnen für Ihre Hilfe. Ich hoffe, daß ich möglichst schnell einen neuen Paß bekomme, da ich übermorgen schon nach England zurückfliegen muß.

Fußnote

1 Polizeistationen sind mit einem blauen Schild mit weißer Schrift und einem weiteren Schild neben der Eingangstür gekennzeichnet. In vielen Fällen befindet sich neben der Tür eine Sprechanlage. In Deutschland gibt es nur die Schutzpolizei— grünbeige Uniformen. Sie ist sowohl Verkehrspolizei als auch für die Beschwerden der Bürger zuständig.

2 Da die Polizeistationen Tag und Nacht besetzt sind, bietet dies auch die Möglichkeit jederzeit eine Auskunft zu erhalten.

Notes

1 Police stations have a large blue sign with *POLIZEI* written in white letters. Another sign is beside the door. Very often there is an intercom at the door, before you can get in. Germany has got only one police force—the *Schutzpolizei*. The police wear green and beige uniforms with white or green hats.

2 If you need help or information at any time, ask at a police station; it will be open day and night.

Unterwegs

An der Tankstelle

TANKWART	Guten Morgen!
• FAHRERIN	1 Guten Morgen! *Ich brauche Benzin.*
TANKWART	2 *Benzin oder Super?*
• FAHRERIN	Super. Bitte volltanken, und würden Sie bitte den Ölstand nachprüfen?
TANKWART	Wird gemacht. So, der Tank ist voll. Bitte öffnen Sie die Motorhaube, damit ich den Ölstand nachprüfen kann ... Es ist alles in Ordnung.
• FAHRERIN	3 Wo kann ich den *Reifendruck* überprüfen?
TANKWART	Da vorne ist ein Druckmeßgerät.
• FAHRERIN	Was habe ich zu zahlen?
TANKWART	Fünfzig Liter Super macht zweiundsechzig Mark fünfzig.

Panne auf der Autobahn

AUTOBAHNM.	4 *Hier ist die Autobahnmeisterei.*
• FAHRER	Ich habe eine Autopanne. Können Sie mir helfen?
AUTOBAHNM.	5 Jawohl. *Wo befinden Sie sich?*
• FAHRER	Ich stehe mit meinem Wagen bei Kilometer 36 auf der A3 in Richtung Köln.

AUTOBAHNM.	Um welchen Fahrzeugtyp handelt es sich? Wissen Sie, was mit Ihrem Wagen los ist?
● FAHRER	Es ist ein Austin-Maxi, und ich glaube, es liegt am Verteilerfinger.
AUTOBAHNM.	Ein Fahrer ist bereits unterwegs. Gehen Sie bitte zu Ihrem Fahrzeug zurück.
● FAHRER	Danke sehr.

Nach dem Weg fragen

● FAHRERIN	Guten Tag! Können Sie mir bitte helfen? Ich suche das Rathaus.
JUNGE	6 Aber gern, meine Dame. Sie fahren jetzt weiter die Umgehungsstraße entlang. *An der 4. Ampel* ordnen Sie sich bitte links ein und biegen ab.
● FAHRERIN	Wie heißt die Straße, in der ich mich dann befinde?
JUNGE	Goethestraße. Diese fahren Sie dann etwa 500m bis zu der großen Kreuzung. Dort biegen Sie dann rechts ab. Diese Straße, die Frankfurter Straße, führt bis auf den Rathausplatz und zum Rathaus.
● FAHRERIN	Vielen Dank!

Autovermietung 7

ANGESTELLTE	Guten Tag! Sie wünschen, bitte?
• HERR PARKER	Ich möchte gern einen Wagen mieten.
ANGESTELLTE	Ja gern. Haben Sie einen besonderen Wunsch welches Fabrikat und Modell es sein soll?
• HERR PARKER	Wenn es möglich ist einen Audi 80 mit Automatik. Ich fahre selbst dieses Auto zu Hause und fühle mich sicherer, wenn ich dieses Fahrzeug nehme.
ANGESTELLTE	Ja, dieses Auto kann ich Ihnen vermieten. Wie lange wollen Sie den P.K.W. fahren?
• HERR PARKER	Nur heute.
ANGESTELLTE	8 Dann kostet es achtundsechzig DM Leihgebühr und die Kosten für das Benzin. Darf ich noch Ihren Paß und Führerschein sehen? . . . *Der Wagen ist voll versichert.* Hier sind die Fahrzeugunterlagen. Gute Fahrt und auf Wiedersehen.
• HERR PARKER	Vielen Dank und auf Wiedersehen.

Fußnote

1 Die deutsche Tankeinheit ist Liter (l). Eine große Zahl von Tankstellen in Deutschland sind inzwischen Selbstbedienungs-tankstellen, an denen man selbst tanken muß—eine Ausnahme bilden hier nur die Autobahntankstellen.

2 Die Tankstellen bieten Normalbenzin, Super- und Dieselkraftstoff an.

3 Die Meßeinheit, in der der Reifendruck gemessen wird heißt atü.

4 Notrufsäulen (gelb) gibt es auf allen Autobahnen und den großeren Bundesstraßen in regelmäßigen Abständen. Ist keine Rufsäule in Sichtweite, so orientiert man sich an den weiß—schwarzen Begrenzungspfählen, Ein kleiner schwarzer Pfeil am oberen Ende zeigt die kürzeste Entfernung zur nächsten Rufsäule an.

5 Beim Öffnen des Gerätes sieht man im Innern ein Schild, auf dem der Standort der Säule genau angegeben ist.

6 Auf Umgehungsstraßen und Straßen mit einem hohen Verkehrsaufkommen besteht die "Grüne Welle". Vorschaltampeln mit Geschwindigkeitsangaben vor den Kreuzungen zeigen dem Autofahrer an, wie schnell er fahren darf, um immer grün zu haben.

7 Neben den Zweigstellen der bekannten Auto-Miet-Unternehmen vermitteln viele Tankstellen PKW's. Hinweisschilder stehen an den Tankstellen.

8 Die Mietwagen sind haftpflichtversichert und haben eine Vollkasko-Versicherung mit 1000 DM Selbstbeteiligung.

Notes

1 Remember that you will be buying petrol in litres. Most of the German filling-stations are self-service except those on the motorway *(Autobahn)*.

2 Petrol is graded as *Benzin* (ordinary, 2 or 3 stars), and *Super* (4 stars). There is also Diesel.

3 Tyre pressure is measured in "atü" (*Atmosphärenüberdruck*, absolute pressure).

4 Yellow emergency telephones are installed on the autobahns (A + number) and on the more important *Bundesstraßen* or main routes (B + number), at regular intervals. If you cannot see an emergency telephone, look at the black and white signposts. At the top there is a small black arrow, which points in the direction of the nearest telephone.

5 When you open the telephone box, you'll see a sign telling you exactly where you are.

6 On ring-roads and other busy roads traffic lights are linked. The speed you must drive to go through all the other traffic lights on green is displayed at the lights before the cross-roads.

7 As well as the branches of the well-known car-hire firms, many petrol stations rent out cars. There are notices advising this at the petrol stations.

8 The hire-car has got a liability insurance and a comprehensive insurance. The customer pays the first 1000 DM in the event of accident or damage to the car. The rest is paid by the insurance company.

Im Restaurant

KELLNERIN		Guten Abend, die Herrschaften.
● MARTIN	1	Guten Abend. Mein Name ist Gaumert. *Ich habe einen Tisch für drei Personen bestellt.*
KELLNERIN		In ein paar Minuten wird Ihr Tisch frei sein. Können Sie ein wenig warten? Er wird gerade neu gedeckt.
● MARTIN		Ja, natürlich. Wir werden inzwischen an der Bar einen Drink nehmen. Was möchtest du trinken, Stephanie?
STEPHANIE		Ich möchte einen trockenen Sherry.
PETER		Für mich einen Malzwhisky.
● MARTIN		Und für mich einen Martini Bianco.
STEPHANIE		Du hast aber ein gemütliches Restaurant für unser Wiedersehen ausgesucht, Martin. Mir gefällt es hier sehr gut. Dir auch, Peter?
PETER		Ja, ich finde es sehr stilvoll, alles alte Möbel. Dadurch entsteht eine besondere Atmosphäre.
● MARTIN		Wenn man sich nach vier Jahren wieder einmal sieht, dann muß man ja schon etwas Besonderes auswählen.

. . . .

KELLNERIN		Der Tisch ist nun frei, mein Herr. Bitte hier entlang. Hier ist die Karte. Was möchten Sie trinken?
● MARTIN	2	Haben Sie *offene Weine*?

KELLNERIN	Ja, einen Schoppen Weißwein oder Rotwein. Bei dem Weißwein können Sie wählen zwischen Rhein-, oder Moselwein.
• MARTIN	Ich möchte 1/4 l. Mosel.
PETER	Und wir nehmen 1/2 l. Rotwein.

. . . .

KELLNERIN	3	So, die Getränke. 1/4 l. Mosel für Sie und 1/2 l. Rotwein für Sie. *Haben Sie schon die Speisen gewählt?*
• MARTIN		Ja, ich hätte gerne eine Zwiebelsuppe als Vorspeise und dann Rostbraten mit Pommes frites und Salat.
STEPHANIE		Ich möchte eine Königinpastete und dann ein Cordon bleu mit Kartoffelkroketten und Gemüse.
PETER		Mir bringen Sie bitte einen Geflügelsalat als Vorspeise und dann das Rehragout mit Rotkohl und Kartoffelklößen.
KELLNERIN		In Ordnung.

. . . .

KELLNERIN	Ich hoffe, es hat Ihnen geschmeckt!
PETER	Ja, danke, es war ausgezeichnet.
KELLNERIN	Wünschen Sie noch eine Nachspeise?
• MARTIN	Ja, ich hätte gerne ein Eis mit Sahne und heißen Himbeeren.
PETER	Und ich einen Obstsalat. Stephanie, wie ist es mit dir?
STEPHANIE	Nein danke, nichts mehr, ich bin satt. Aber eine Tasse Kaffee könnte ich noch vertragen.

• MARTIN	Na, ich hoffe nach vier Jahren hat euch die deutsche Küche wieder mal geschmeckt.
STEPHANIE	Ja, sehr, das Essen war ausgezeichnet und der Wein war auch vorzüglich.
• MARTIN	Glaubst du, daß es große Unterschiede zwischen der englischen Küche und der deutschen Küche gibt?
STEPHANIE	Unterschiede gibt es in jedem Land, so auch zwischen der englischen und deutschen Küche. Aber das ist ja nicht schlimm. Man sollte ja gerade auch einmal die Eigenarten und Bräuche des Landes probieren, in dem man ist. Stell dir vor, auf der ganzen Welt gäbe es die gleichen Gerichte.
PETER	Das wäre ja schlimm!
• MARTIN	Fräulein, die Rechnung bitte.
KELLNERIN	Jawohl, mein Herr, hier ist sie. Wünschen Sie eine Quittung?
• MARTIN	4 Nein, das ist nicht nötig. Vielen Dank. So . . . *der Rest ist für Sie.*
KELLNERIN	Vielen Dank. Auf Wiedersehen.

Fußnote

1 Um bei sehr guten Restaurants Wartezeiten zu vermeiden, ist es sinnvoll, vorher einen Tisch zu bestellen.

2 Unter "offene Weine" versteht man die Möglichkeit nur 1/4 l. oder 1/2 l. Wein einer Flasche serviert zu bekommen. Man braucht nicht die ganze Flasche zu bestellen.
Bei den offenen Weinen handelt es sich in den meisten Fällen um leichte Weine.

3 Während Mittags die Speiserestaurants preiswerte Menüs (Suppe oder Vorspeise, Hauptmahlzeit, Dessert) anbieten, ißt man abends à la carte.

4   Die Rechnung beinhaltet sowohl die Mehrwertsteuer als auch ein Bedienungsgeld. Es ist jedoch empfehlenswert, dem Ober ein weiteres Trinkgeld zu geben.

Notes

1   At some of the better restaurants you might have to wait for a table, so it is advisable to reserve one beforehand.

2   *Offene Weine* means you can buy a quarter- or half-litre carafe of wine, rather than a whole bottle. "Open" wines of this kind are usually very light.

3   Whereas at lunchtime restaurants offer special menus (soup, main course, dessert), in the evening you eat à la carte.

4   The bill always includes VAT and service, but most people leave a further tip.

At the hotel reception desk

RECEPTION   Good morning, sir. What can I do for you?

GUEST   Good morning. I'd like a double room.

RECEPTION   How long do you intend to stay?

GUEST   For three nights, please.

RECEPTION   Unfortunately we have no double rooms with bath free at the moment. We have a lot of guests. But I could offer you a double with shower.

GUEST   That's alright by me.

RECEPTION   A double room costs 60 Marks per night.

GUEST   Per person?

RECEPTION   No sir, 60 DM is the price for two people.

GUEST   Good, that's alright then. Is breakfast included in the price?

RECEPTION   Of course sir.

GUEST   Right, I'll take the double room with shower.

RECEPTION   It's room number 76, fourth floor. Here is your key.

GUEST   Where is the lift? Our luggage is very heavy.

RECEPTION   Just to the right of the main entrance. I'll call a porter for you. Franz! Please help this gentleman to room 76.

GUEST   The luggage is outside in the car. I'll go and get it.

RECEPTION	Franz will help you, sir. Oh, one moment please. When would you like breakfast?
GUEST	Is it served in the bedroom?
RECEPTION	Yes sir, or downstairs in the dining-room, whichever you prefer.
GUEST	Please serve it to us at 9 o'clock, in our room.
RECEPTION	Certainly sir. And what would you like to drink? Coffee, tea or chocolate?
GUEST	White coffee for me and tea without milk for my wife.
RECEPTION	Right, I've noted that. I hope you have a pleasant stay in our hotel.
	. . . .
GUEST	Franz, would you be so kind and take the two big suitcases, then I'll bring the other luggage.
FRANZ	Yes, of course. Please follow me to the lift. Your room is on the fourth floor.
GUEST	Is this the only lift in the hotel?
FRANZ	No sir. If you want to get into the restaurant or bar take the lift at the end of the corridor. It leads straight into the restaurant. Well, here we are; room 76. I hope you have a good time.
GUEST	Thank you very much. And that's for you.
FRANZ	Thank you.

In the cafe

CUSTOMER	Waiter!
WAITER	Yes, madam?
CUSTOMER	I'd like a pot of coffee with milk and a cake. What sort do you have?
WAITER	There is a buffet over there; please go and choose what you want. You'll then be given a ticket which you pass on to me, and I'll bring you your cake.
CUSTOMER	Thank you.

. . . .

WAITER	Have you chosen something?
CUSTOMER	Yes, here is my ticket.
WAITER	Your cake will come at once.

. . . .

WAITER	Here is your pot of coffee and a piece of strawberry tart with cream.
CUSTOMER	Would you bring me a packet of cigarettes, please?
WAITER	Yes, what sort do you like?
CUSTOMER	Bring me twenty Rothmans—and the bill, please.

. . . .

WAITER	You had a pot of coffee for 3 DM, a piece of strawberry tart with cream 2.50 DM, a packet of cigarettes 3 DM. That makes 8.50 DM altogether.
CUSTOMER	Is service included?
WAITER	Yes, thank you.

At the counter

ASSISTANT	What can I do for you?
CUSTOMER	What are these delicious biscuits you have here?
ASSISTANT	They are almond biscuits. 125g cost 2 DM.
CUSTOMER	Oh, let me have 250g of them please.
ASSISTANT	Here they are. Anything else?
CUSTOMER	Oh yes—I would also like a box of chocolates. Have you any filled with brandy?
ASSISTANT	Yes, these here. They cost 8.50 DM.
CUSTOMER	Please gift wrap them for me. Here's the 12.50 DM.
ASSISTANT	Here are the biscuits and the chocolates. Many thanks and goodbye.
CUSTOMER	Goodbye.

At the bank

MR. SMITH	Good morning! Can I change foreign money here?
EMPLOYEE	Not at my counter, sir, but my colleague over there will help you.
MR. SMITH	Good morning, I'd like to change some money.
EMPLOYEE	Have you got cash, cheques or travellers' cheques?

MR. SMITH	Travellers' cheques. Here are two cheques for £50 each. Please change then into Deutsche Marks.
EMPLOYEE	One moment please. I'll have a look at the exchange rate . . . You'll get 4.05 DM for £1.
MR. SMITH	Fine, here they are.
EMPLOYEE	Please sign the cheques here. You'll get 405 DM for them.
MR. SMITH	Please let me have 10 DM and 20 DM notes.
EMPLOYEE	Is that alright?
MR. SMITH	Yes, but please change this 10 Mark note into coins so that I can make a phone call. Thank you very much. Good morning.

At the baker's

BAKER	Good morning, Mrs. Müller.
CUSTOMER	Good morning, Mr. Meier.
BAKER	What can I do for you?
CUSTOMER	Ten fresh rolls, please.
BAKER	Here you are; the rolls are very fresh, not from the freezer. Anything else?

CUSTOMER	Wait a moment . . . oh yes, one pound of brown bread, but thin slices, please, and half a pound of butter. I think that's all. Oh, what are your special offers this week?
BAKER	Here's a new brand of coffee, only 7.95 DM a pound.
CUSTOMER	Is it good?
BAKER	Well, I haven't tried it myself yet; you know, my wife likes her brand above all others.
CUSTOMER	Then I'll leave it. Anyway, I must be careful with my money; it is only the 25th and I haven't much left. How much is that altogther?
BAKER	The rolls are 20 pfennigs each, the brown bread is 1.69 DM and the butter 1.89 DM . . . wait a minute, that's 5.58 DM altogether.
CUSTOMER	Here's 6 DM.
BAKER	Here's your change, 42 pfennigs; thank you very much, Mrs. Müller. Goodbye.
CUSTOMER	Goodbye, Mr. Meier.

At the station

At the ticket office

MARTIN   Good morning. I'd like a single to Cologne.

EMPLOYEE   First or second class, sir?

MARTIN   Second, please. Can you tell me when the next train leaves? I must be in Cologne at 12 o'clock, because my friends arrive at Cologne station at 12.30.

EMPLOYEE   The next train leaves at 11.08. You'll get to Cologne with time to spare.

MARTIN   Which platform does my train leave from?

EMPLOYEE   Platform 2. Here is your ticket.

MARTIN   Thank you.

At Cologne station

MARTIN   Can you tell me which platform the 12.30 train from Ostend arrives at?

EMPLOYEE   One moment please. The train arrives at platform 7a/b. But it's been announced that it will be ten minutes late.

MARTIN   It doesn't matter. I'll buy a newspaper first.

At the kiosk

MARTIN	Good morning. Have you got foreign newspapers?
ASSISTANT	What would you like? French, English, Turkish, Spanish, Italian, Dutch or Danish?
MARTIN	I'd like an English paper.
ASSISTANT	Well, I can offer you the Daily Express, Daily Mail, Financial Times or the Daily Mirror.
MARTIN	Please give me the Daily Express. And can you tell me where platform 7a/b is?
ASSISTANT	Go along there and turn right at the telephone box. You will find the sign 7a/b on the left-hand wall.
MARTIN	Thank you. Oh, the loudspeaker is just announcing my train. I must hurry. 'Bye.

On the platform

MARTIN	Hello Stephanie, hello Peter!
PETER & STEPHANIE	Hello Martin!
MARTIN	I'm so happy to see you again. Have you had a pleasant journey?
PETER	Yes thank you. The journey by rail was very interesting but it took a very long time.
MARTIN	And how was the Channel crossing, Stephanie?

STEPHANIE	It was great, Martin. The sun came out and we had a calm sea.
MARTIN	Well, let's go home then. Have you got your luggage?
STEPHANIE	Yes, everything's okay.

At the post office

CLERK	Yes please?
CUSTOMER	I'd like a stamp for this postcard to England, please. How much is it?
CLERK	60 pfennig, madam.
CUSTOMER	And how much is a letter to England?
CLERK	80 pfennig to England. To all other countries of the Common Market except Ireland and Denmark it costs 60 pfennig.
CUSTOMER	Really? Then please give me a 60 pfennig stamp and an 80 pfennig stamp.
CLERK	Anything else, madam?
CUSTOMER	Oh yes, I nearly forgot. I'd like to make a phone call to London, please. Is it possible to do so from here?
CLERK	Yes, you can. Please give me the telephone number and go into booth number 3. When the telephone rings, please lift the receiver. After finishing your call come back to me to pay the bill.
CUSTOMER	How much is a three minute call?
CLERK	One minute costs you about 2.30 DM.

. . . .

CUSTOMER	Sorry, I couldn't get through. I'll try again in an hour's time.
CLERK	We will have closed by then. But you can use a call box to phone England.
CUSTOMER	That's fine. Can you give me the code number?
CLERK	You dial 0044 for England; then the code for the town. In doing so please leave out the 0 of the town's code number, and then finally you dial the subscriber's number.
CUSTOMER	Thank you very much, and goodbye.

In the shoe shop

ASSISTANT	Good afternoon, sir, can I help you?
CUSTOMER	I'd like a pair of comfortable but not too expensive shoes, please.
ASSISTANT	Well, please have a look on these shelves. Perhaps you'll find something you like. What size do you take?
CUSTOMER	43.
ASSISTANT	Here are the shelves with size 43. If you don't like any of those, I'll show you some others.
	. . . .
ASSISTANT	Take a seat, sir. Now I'll show you several other styles. Here I have a very nice pair of shoes with rubber soles, but only in black.
CUSTOMER	Oh yes, that one is very comfortable. May I try the left one too? How much are they?

ASSISTANT	Here's the left one. They are 98 DM.
CUSTOMER	It's rather expensive, but I do like them. I'll take them.
ASSISTANT	If you'd like to come to the cash desk, please. Would you like a special cleaning cream for them?
CUSTOMER	No thank you, I've got shoe polish at home.
ASSISTANT	98 DM, please.
CUSTOMER	Here's 100 DM.
ASSISTANT	And here's your 2 DM change. Goodbye and thank you very much.

At the butcher's

CUSTOMER	Good morning!
BUTCHER	Good morning. Can I help you, madam?
CUSTOMER	I'd like 1½lbs of stewing meat.
BUTCHER	Beef or pork?
CUSTOMER	Half each please. And I'd like four cutlets please.
BUTCHER	Anything else?
CUSTOMER	Yes, I need some cold meat. Half a pound of liver sausage, a quarter of salami and half of boiled ham.
BUTCHER	Here they are. Anything else?
CUSTOMER	I'd like some meat for a barbecue. Can you recommend anything?
BUTCHER	Oh yes. I've some very delicious sausages for grilling here, and of course steaks too.

CUSTOMER	Then please give me ten sausages and five steaks.
BUTCHER	Anything else?
CUSTOMER	No thank you, that's all.
BUTCHER	That is 42.20 DM, madam.
CUSTOMER	Here is 50 DM.
BUTCHER	And here is your change, 7.80 DM. Thank you very much, goodbye.
CUSTOMER	Goodbye.

In the chemist's and at the dentist

At the chemist's

CUSTOMER	Good morning.
PHARMACIST	Good morning. How can I help you?
CUSTOMER	My wife has dreadful toothache. What can we do for it?
PHARMACIST	I'll give you this packet of pain-killing tablets. She must take one of them now and another one in four hours' time. If the pain is not eased, she should go to a dentist.
CUSTOMER	Can you tell me which dentist is available?
PHARMACIST	Yes, I'll give you a list of the dentists who are on duty.
CUSTOMER	How much do I owe you?
PHARMACIST	5.25 DM for the tablets.
CUSTOMER	Thank you very much, and goodbye.
PHARMACIST	Goodbye.

At the dentist

ASSISTANT	Mrs. Smith, would you come in please?
DENTIST	Good morning, Mrs. Smith. How can I help you?
MRS. SMITH	I've an awful toothache. Last night I lost a filling.
DENTIST	Let your head go right back. Can you open your mouth a little wider?
MRS. SMITH	It's the second molar on the top right.
DENTIST	Is it this one?
MRS. SMITH	Yes, it's the one you've just touched.
DENTIST	I'm afraid it will hurt a bit. Sorry, that's rather a tender spot, but I'll soon be finished with the drill. There that's over; now I can put the filling in. Would you rinse your mouth, please?
MRS. SMITH	I'm feeling better already!
DENTIST	Please don't eat anything for the next three hours. I'll have a quick look at the other teeth. Here is one that may give you trouble soon. When you are back at home, go to your dentist without delay.
MRS. SMITH	Oh yes, I'll do that. Thank you very much.
DENTIST	Goodbye, Mrs. Smith.
MRS. SMITH	Goodbye, doctor.

In the afternoon at the chemist's

PHARMACIST   Good afternoon. Is your wife feeling better now?

CUSTOMER   No, we had to go to the dentist. He had to fill the tooth and gave me a prescription.

PHARMACIST   Oh, I see. Another stronger pain-killer and something to prevent infection. You can only get such medicines with a prescription. Here are your medicines . . . that's 22.50 DM. Do you need anything else?

CUSTOMER   Yes, I've just noticed that my tablets which I have to take regularly have run out. They are tablets to counter high blood pressure.

PHARMACIST   Can you tell me the name of the medicine?

CUSTOMER   Yes, here is the empty box.

PHARMACIST   That is a foreign preparation, that's not sold under this name in Germany. But I can supply you with a German medicine. It has the same ingredients as yours—only another name.

CUSTOMER   That would help me a great deal. What do I have to pay?

PHARMACIST   It is 7.75 DM for this. That's 30.25 DM altogether.

CUSTOMER   Many thanks for your help, and goodbye.

PHARMACIST   Goodbye, and I wish your wife a speedy recovery.

A sightseeing tour of Cologne

In the tourist office

ASSISTANT	Good morning, can I help you?
TOURIST	I would like to book a sightseeing tour.
ASSISTANT	Yes of course. It starts in an hour and the coach leaves from over there at the coach station.
TOURIST	How much is it?
ASSISTANT	10 DM please.

On the coach

GUIDE	Good morning ladies and gentlemen! My name is Gerd Radandt. I would like to show you our beautiful city of Cologne in the next two hours. If you have questions during the tour, I'll gladly answer them for you.
	(The coach sets off)
GUIDE	Ladies and gentlemen, while we are driving along the Rhine embankment I'll tell you something about Cologne, one of the oldest towns in Germany. Cologne was founded by the Romans, before the birth of Christ, as a base on the Rhine. Under the Emperor Claudius in 50 A.D. it became the centre of Roman Germania and was given the name Colonia Agrippinensis.

TOURIST	Are there any traces of this Roman past today?
GUIDE	Yes. In the last few decades a lot of buildings of Roman origin have been discovered. The area round Cologne cathedral was a Roman settlement and a lot of foundations and walls are still in good condition. So are mosaics, columns, towers and many other objects. A comprehensive collection can be seen in the "Römisch-Germanische Museum", next to the cathedral.
TOURIST	Has Cologne other important and famous museums?
GUIDE	Yes, of course. There are some other museums, and also a museum of folklore.
	. . . .
GUIDE	On the right you can now see the old centre of Cologne. The beautiful house fronts are medieval in style. The "Altstadt" (Old Town) as it is called, is a very popular meeting-place with its many restaurants and pubs. The opening of the Cologne street carnival takes place here in the "Alter Markt" (Old Marketplace) every year in February at Carnival time.
TOURIST	Isn't there always a big carnival procession?
GUIDE	That's right. On "Rosenmontag" (Rose Monday), the climax of the Rhine carnival, there is a procession through the streets of Cologne which is five to six kilometres long.

Now we turn into one of Cologne's ring roads, which marks the limits of medieval Cologne. Here you can still see a lot of city gates from that period. From the ring road nearly all roads lead into the centre, to the cathedral.

TOURIST   What's that tower over there?

GUIDE   That is the new Post Office Tower, which was built only recently. Cologne people call the tower "Colonius".

We are now going towards the city centre, to Cologne cathedral, passing through the banking district. It is the biggest Gothic building in Germany. Building was started in 1248 and the cathedral was not finished until 1880.

TOURIST   Can you advise us where to go shopping?

GUIDE   One of Cologne's two big shopping streets, the Hohe Straße, begins in front of the cathedral and ends where it meets the other busy shopping street, Schildergasse. At the beginning of the Hohe Straße is the "Heinzelmännchen-Brunnen" (Pixie Fountain) which was inspired by an old Cologne legend.

We are now coming back to the coach station. In front of us is the Rhine again.

TOURIST   You can see a lot of passenger boats on the Rhine. Where can you go to on them?

GUIDE   In summer there are regular river trips between Cologne and the towns up-river like Bonn, Königswinter and

Koblenz. You can also join one of the evening dance-parties on a boat.

I hope you've enjoyed the sightseeing tour, and I wish you a pleasant stay in our cathedral city. Goodbye.

At the police station

POLICEMAN	Yes please, can I help you?
MR. RUSTON	Yes, you can help me. I've lost my passport.
POLICEMAN	Please, come into this room. Sit down please and answer the following questions. What's your name.
MR. RUSTON	Michael Ruston.
POLICEMAN	Where do you live?
MR. RUSTON	281 Edenhill Road, London.
POLICEMAN	When were you born, and where?
MR. RUSTON	The 1st of June 1948, in Southampton.
POLICEMAN	Please put your signature under your declaration of loss.
MR. RUSTON	Okay, but what must I do now?
POLICEMAN	I'll give you the address of the British Consulate in Düsseldorf. You must go there and present this statement. Then you'll get a provisional passport.
MR. RUSTON	Thank you for your help. I hope I'll get a new passport soon because I have to fly back to England in two days.

On the road

At the petrol station

ATTENDANT	Good morning!
DRIVER	Good morning. I need some petrol.
ATTENDANT	Ordinary or 'super'?
DRIVER	'Super'. Please fill up the tank. And would you check the oil please?
ATTENDANT	Yes madam. Well, the tank is full. Would you please open the bonnet so that I can check the oil . . . It's okay.
DRIVER	Where can I check the tyre pressure?
ATTENDANT	Over there, there's a tyre pressure gauge.
DRIVER	What do I have to pay?
ATTENDANT	50 litres of 'super', that'll be 62.50 DM.

A breakdown on the motorway—phoning for help

SERVICE MAN	This is the Motorway Emergency Centre ("Autobahnmeisterei").
DRIVER	I have broken down. Can you help me?
SERVICE MAN	Yes sir. Where exactly are you?
DRIVER	I am on the autobahn A3 to Cologne, at kilometre 36.
SERVICE MAN	What kind of a car do you have and do you know what is wrong with it?

DRIVER	It's an Austin Maxi, and I think it is the distributor arm.
SERVICE MAN	A man is on the way. Please go back to your vehicle.
DRIVER	Thank you very much.

Asking the way

DRIVER	Hello! Can you help me please? I'm looking for the Rathaus (Town Hall).
BOY	Yes of course, madam. You continue along the ringroad. At the fourth set of traffic lights you go into the left hand lane and turn left.
DRIVER	What's the name of the road I shall then be in?
BOY	Goethestraße. You go along Goethestraße for about 500 metres until you reach a big junction. There you turn right. That is the Frankfurter Straße; it runs straight to the Rathausplatz and the Rathaus.
DRIVER	Thank you very much!

Renting a car

EMPLOYEE	Good morning, can I help you?
MR. PARKER	I would like to hire a car.
EMPLOYEE	Yes, of course. Have you any preference to what make and model it should be?

MR. PARKER	If it's possible, an Audi 80 automatic. I drive this car at home and will feel safer in one now.
EMPLOYEE	Oh yes, I can let you have one. How long do you want to drive the car for?
MR. PARKER	Only today.
EMPLOYEE	Then it costs 68 DM to rent the car, and the cost of the petrol. May I see your passport and driving licence... The car is fully insured. Here are the documents for the vehicle. Have a good trip, and goodbye.
MR. PARKER	Thank you very much. Goodbye.

In the restaurant

WAITRESS	Good evening gentlemen, madam.
MARTIN	Good evening. My name is Gaumert. I've ordered a table for three.
WAITRESS	There will be a table free in a few minutes. Can you wait a moment? It is just being relaid.
MARTIN	Yes, of course. In the meantime we'll have a drink at the bar. What would you like, Stephanie?
STEPHANIE	I'd like a dry sherry.
PETER	Malt whisky for me.
MARTIN	And for me a Martini bianco.
STEPHANIE	You've certainly chosen a lovely restaurant for our get-together, Martin. I like it very much here. Do you like it too, Peter?

PETER	Yes, I like the style. All this old furniture gives it a special atmosphere.
MARTIN	When you see each other again after four years, you have to choose something special.
	. . . .
WAITRESS	The table is free now, sir. This way please. Here's the menu . . . what would you like to drink?
MARTIN	Have you a house wine?
WAITRESS	Yes, either white or red. In the white wines you may choose between Rhine and Moselle.
MARTIN	I'd like a quarter-litre of Moselle.
PETER	And we'd like a half-litre of red wine.
	. . . .
WAITRESS	So, your drinks . . . a quarter-litre Moselle for you and a half-litre of red wine for you. Have you chosen what to eat yet?
MARTIN	Yes, I'll have onion soup to start with, and then roast beef with chips and salad.
STEPHANIE	I'd like a vol-au-vent and then a 'Cordon Bleu' with croquette potatoes and vegetables.
PETER	Bring me a poultry salad to start with please, and then venison casserole with red cabbage and potato dumplings.
WAITRESS	Very well.
	. . . .

WAITRESS	I hope you enjoyed it.
PETER	Yes thank you, it was excellent.
WAITRESS	Would you like something to finish with?
MARTIN	Yes please, I'd like an ice with hot raspberries and cream.
PETER	And a fruit salad for me. Stephanie, what do you want?
STEPHANIE	Nothing, thank you. I am full. But I could drink a cup of coffee.
MARTIN	Well, I hope you've enjoyed German cooking again after four years.
STEPHANIE	Yes, very much. The dinner was excellent, and the wine too.
MARTIN	Do you think there is a great difference between English and German cooking?
STEPHANIE	There are differences in every country, so too between English and German cooking. But that isn't a bad thing. One should really try to learn something about the peculiarities and customs of the country one is in. Imagine if there were the same meals all over the world.
PETER	That would be awful!
	. . . .
MARTIN	Waitress, the bill please.
WAITRESS	Certainly sir, here it is. Do you want a receipt?
MARTIN	No, that's not necessary. Many thanks. There . . . keep the change.
WAITRESS	Thank you very much sir. Goodbye.

Further publications from

hugo

The 'Three Months' series
Teach yourself a new language in three months using the
famous Hugo method with easy imitated pronunciation.

Audio courses
The 'Three Months' books with cassettes, so you can
hear the language as it is spoken.

The 'Speak Today' series
A cassette and a book for improving your colloquial
ability in a foreign language.

Verb books
Invaluable reference books with complete lists of verbs,
with their formation explained.

Travel packs
One phrase book with a cassette, so you can practise the
phrases before your trip!

Phrase books
Useful phrases for all essential situations abroad, plus a
menu guide and mini-dictionary.

Pocket dictionaries
Over 22,000 words in each, with imitated pronunciation.

Write to us for prices and more details, or phone 01-837
0486/7/8.
Hugo's Language Books Ltd, 104 Judd Street, London
WC1H 9NF.